The Complete Mediterranean Diet Cookbook

Quick, Delicious and Super-Amazing Meals for Everyday Enjoyment including a 14-Day Meal Plan

Matthew A. Harrington

ISBN - 9798849457338

TABLE OF CONTENTS

EXCLUSIVE BONUS

40 Weight Loss Recipes

&

14 Days Meal Plan

Scan the QR-Code and receive
the FREE download:

Introduction

Changing your diet is never simple, especially if you have to cut out on convenience items like takeouts and processed foods. However, eating a Mediterranean-style diet is affordable, delicious, and extremely healthy.

Compared to other diets, the Mediterranean "diet" is unique. For starters, it's been around much longer; locals have been eating this way for centuries. Plus, it has been gaining popularity internationally for almost 50 years due to its longevity.

Two essential diet components are engaging in daily physical activity and dining with people. Together, they can significantly impact your mental and emotional well-being and help you develop a deep appreciation for the benefits of consuming wholesome meals.

Remember: Moving from pepperoni and pasta to fish and avocados can take some work, but if you do, you'll be on the road to a healthier and longer life.

History of the Mediterranean Diet

Two thousand years ago, the three staples of the Mediterranean diet — olive trees for producing olives and olive oil, wheat for making bread, and grapevines for producing grapes and wine — were the bread and butter of the Phoenicians, Greeks, and Romans.

The Romans also ate a variety of vegetables, such as onions, lettuce, leeks, cabbage, carrots, turnips, asparagus, celery, and artichokes, as well as a wide range of fruits, such as figs, pears, apples, cherries, plums, peaches, apricots, and citrus fruits. Other popular foods back then were chestnuts, walnuts, and almonds.

The Moors' occupation of the Spanish or Iberian Peninsula in the seventh century A.D. marked a significant development in the Mediterranean diet. They spread rice, lemons, eggplants, saffron, and other spices, which later expanded throughout the Mediterranean basin, leading to the development of the Mediterranean diet we know today.

Health Benefits: The Mediterranean Diet

When combined with regular exercise, a traditional Mediterranean diet — rich in fresh fruits, vegetables, nuts, fish, and olive oil — can lower your chance of developing major mental and physical health issues by:

Preventing Strokes and Heart Disease

Limiting your consumption of refined grains, processed foods, and red meat while promoting red wine consumption instead of hard liquor are aspects of the Mediterranean diet that can help avoid heart disease and stroke.

Decreasing the Risk of Parkinson's Disease

The high antioxidant content in the Mediterranean diet can shield cells from the harmful effects of oxidative stress, reducing the likelihood of developing Parkinson's disease by 50%.

Preserving Your Agility

The nutrients you get from a Mediterranean diet may reduce the likelihood of developing muscle weakness and other frailty indicators by roughly 70% if you're an older adult.

Benefiting People with Arthritis

The Mediterranean diet features many anti-inflammatory foods like tomatoes, olive oil, and green vegetables that reduce inflammation and decrease the pain experienced by people with arthritis, which is an inflammatory disease.

Encouraging Exercise

The Mediterranean diet is one of the few eating plans that specifically encourage physical exercise. Given that most adults in America don't exercise enough, this is a good addition. Moreover, frequent exercisers are more likely to choose healthier meals throughout the day.

Interestingly, the Mediterranean diet and exercise may have a mutually beneficial relationship. In a study, researchers discovered that consuming a Mediterranean rather than the standard Western diet may boost your physical performance.[1]

Protecting Against (Some) Cancers

The protection provided by the Mediterranean diet against chronic illnesses like cardiovascular disease, diabetes, and metabolic syndrome is well-known and lauded. But this anti-inflammatory and antioxidant-rich diet may also offer protection against some cancers, such as breast, colorectum, stomach, prostate, and pancreatic cancer.[2]

---

1   https://www.nature.com/articles/s41366-018-0299-3
2   https://www.ncbi.nlm.nih.gov/pmc/articles/PMC4778149/

Allowing for Dietary Preferences

You may adapt the Mediterranean diet to fit your lifestyle, whether vegan, vegetarian, gluten-free, paleo, dairy-free, etc. The diet works best when all the food types it emphasizes are allowed, although you can change it to suit your dietary preferences.

The Mediterranean Diet Is About Healthy Fats, Not Unhealthy Ones

The primary source of additional fat in the Mediterranean diet is olive oil. The monounsaturated fat found in olive oil decreases bad cholesterol (LDL) and total cholesterol. Monounsaturated fat is also present in nuts and seeds.

Omega-3 fatty acids present in this diet are abundant in fatty fish, including mackerel, sardines, herring, albacore tuna, and salmon. These polyunsaturated fat-rich foods help the body fight against inflammation.

Busting Myths Around the Mediterranean Diet

There are many advantages to eating a Mediterranean-style diet, but there are also many myths about using this way of living to live a better, longer life. The myths and realities surrounding the Mediterranean diet are listed below.

Myth 1# Mediterranean Diet Is All About Food

Fact: Yes, food plays a significant role in the diet, but you shouldn't ignore the other aspects of how the Mediterranean people live. They eat meals with people in a comfortable, unhurried setting rather than in front of the television or in a hurry, which may be just as beneficial to your health as the food you consume.

Plus, Mediterranean people participate in many physical activities, such as frequent walks and games like football.

Myth 2# Mediterranean Diet Is High in Fats

Fact: Fat is usually believed to be the killer of heart health and the leading cause of arterial sediments that lead to coronary artery disease. In reality, the reverse is true! Fats in the Mediterranean diet are actually good for the heart and aren't linked to weight gain or ill health.

In a study, compared to participants who were instructed to follow a usual diet, those randomly assigned to consume nuts or olive oil as part of a Mediterranean diet discovered that their health had improved.

Myth 3# The Mediterranean Diet Is Expensive

Fact: The Mediterranean diet is more affordable than serving plates of packaged or processed foods — but only if you're using beans or lentils as your primary source of protein and adhering to larger plants and whole grains.

Myth 4# The Mediterranean Diet Calls for Eating Huge Quantities of Pasta and Bread

Fact: Unlike Americans, most Mediterranean people don't typically eat a massive plate of spaghetti. Instead, pasta is typically served as a side dish with a serving size of 1/2 cup and 1 cup. The remaining items on the plate are salads, vegetables, fish, a modest serving of grass-fed, organic meat, and possibly a slice of bread.

Myth 5# The Mediterranean Diet Is Hard to Follow

Fact: Any wholesome, healthy eating plan can be followed just as easily as the Mediterranean diet. Yes, it will feel challenging at first because you'll be forming new habits, but over time, it'll become easier and almost second nature.

Characteristics of the Mediterranean Diet

The most valuable food type in the Mediterranean Diet is olive oil, which is rich in oleic acid and other antioxidants. It slows the development of coronary heart disease, promotes cholesterol control, slows the development of certain types of cancer, and reduces the effects of free radicals. It's used as the main fat for dressings and frying.

Another essential feature of this diet is the consumption of cereals, which have been shown to have beneficial effects on reducing the risk of ischemic heart disease and some cancers. A typical Mediterranean diet recommends daily consumption of bread, pasta, potatoes, rice, and other foods made with cereals.

Some of the ingredients used in the diet include:

- Olive oil
- Olive
- Wheat
- Lemon
- Wine
- Chickpeas
- Yogurt
- Herbs
- Garlic.

Tips and Tricks: The Mediterranean Diet

A diet is one of the hardest, most challenging transitions for many of us and may take some time to stick. However, there're several ways you can make it easier, such as:

1. Start by substituting a prepared dinner for a fast-food one. For instance, if you're craving chicken wings, try making them the Greek way! Alternatively, try baking them in olive oil if you want sweet potato fries. Simply put, find a healthy homemade substitute for your favorite fast food.

2. Eat more grains, legumes, fruits, and veggies. Every meal should start with the component that forms the Mediterranean diet pyramid.

3. Choose vegetarian dinners like cauliflower, chickpea, and lentil soup whenever possible.

4. Increase your reliance on filling, flavorful salads to make up a sizable percentage of your plate.

5. Consume eggs and dairy. Dairy product consumption has health advantages, such as a decreased risk of diabetes, metabolic syndrome, cardiovascular disease, and obesity. Sadly, according to the U.S.D.A., more than 80% of Americans do not consume the recommended number of dairy products daily. We're not suggesting that processed cheese

be liberally sprinkled on everything. But perhaps, instead of chips for a snack, try low-fat Greek yogurt.

6. Reduce your consumption of fatty red meats significantly. Eat additional lean proteins, such as fish, around twice a week and moderate amounts of poultry. Red meat is still acceptable occasionally but sticks to leaner cuts. In Greece and other Mediterranean nations, lamb is frequently the red meat of choice. You may try moussaka, kofta kebobs, and grilled lamb chops.

How Can You Make the Change?

If you're beginning to feel intimidated by the idea of switching to a Mediterranean diet, here are some ideas to get you started:

- **Eat Vegetables** – Try a straightforward plate of sliced tomatoes, olive oil, and feta cheese crumbles, or top your thin crust pizza with peppers and mushrooms in place of sausage and pepperoni. You can eat many veggies by consuming salads, soups, and crudité platters.

- **Eat Breakfast Every Day** – Starting your day with whole grains, and other fiber-rich foods will keep you pleasantly full for several hours.

- **Consume Fish Twice a Week** – Fish high in omega-3 fatty acids, like tuna, salmon, herring, and sardines, and shellfish, like mussels, oysters, and clams, are good for the heart and brain.

- **Use Healthy Fats** – Extra-virgin olive oil, almonds, olives, sunflower seeds, and avocados are excellent sources of healthy fats for your everyday meals.

EXCLUSIVE BONUS

40 Weight Loss Recipes

&

14 Days Meal Plan

Scan the QR-Code and receive
the FREE download:

Mediterranean Recipes

Recipes for the Mediterranean diet emphasize colorful, high-vegetable, high-fruit, lean protein, and healthy fat foods. These quick and healthy recipes, emphasizing plant-based foods and various seafood, will make you feel great from the inside out!

SHEET PAN BAKED EGGS AND VEGETABLES

The ideal method for preparing breakfast for a large group is eggs and vegetables on a sheet pan! Let's cook sunny-side-up eggs, colorful bell peppers, onions, and a one-pan dinner with strong Mediterranean flavors.

Total time: 20 minutes
Per serving: 143 calories; carbohydrates 2.5g; protein 13.8g; total fat 15.1g

INGREDIENTS

- 1 green bell pepper
- 1 red bell pepper
- 1 medium red onion
- 1 Roma tomato
- 1 punch chopped fresh parsley
- 3-4 cubes of feta cheese
- 1 pinch of salt and black pepper (or to taste)
- 1 teaspoon ground cumin
- 1 to 2 tablespoons virgin olive oil
- 6 large eggs

PREPARATION

1. Preheat the oven to 400°F.

2. Place sliced bell peppers in a bowl, and add cumin, salt, and pepper.

3. Drizzle with extra virgin oil.

4. Transfer the mixture of peppers and onions to a sheet pan and bake for 10 to 15 minutes.

5. Remove the sheet pan from the oven. Make six small, precise slits or openings in the roasted vegetables.

6. Crack an egg into the openings in the vegetables.

7. Bake for two to three minutes or until the egg whites are set.

8. Take the hot sheet pan out of the warm oven, and season the eggs.

9. Add some feta, diced tomatoes, and parsley.

10. Serve fresh.

HUMMUS TOAST

We usually don't realize how much simpler and superior homemade hummus is to store-bought varieties. You can change the toppings according to your taste and enjoy a delicious recipe. This simple hummus toast can be used for breakfast, lunch, or dinner.

Total time: 20 minutes
Per serving: 250 calories; carbohydrates 33g; protein 7g; total fat 11g

INGREDIENTS

- 3 cups cooked chickpeas
- 1 to 2 garlic cloves
- 1 tablespoon of lemon juice
- 1/3 cup tahini paste
- 1/2 teaspoon salt or to taste
- 3-4 ice cubes
- 1-3 tablespoons of hot water

PREPARATION

1. Toss the chickpeas and minced garlic into a food processor and blend until everything combines.

2. Add the ice cubes, salt, lemon juice, and tahini while the processor is still running. Blend for four minutes.

3. Slowly add a little hot water if the consistency is still too thick.

4. Blend till you achieve the ideal silky-smooth consistency.

5. Spread the hummus on toast, or eat it with your favorite vegetable.

ROSEMARY-WALNUT CRUSTED SALMON

Omega-3 fatty acids are abundant in both walnuts and salmon. The fatty acids in these nuts are called alpha-linolenic acid (ALA), an essential fat to include in your diet. Serve this crusted salmon with a quick salad, quinoa or roasted potatoes.

Total time: 20 minutes
Per serving: 222 calories, carbohydrates 4g; protein 24g; total fat 12g

INGREDIENTS

- 1 minced clove of garlic
- 2 teaspoons of Dijon mustard
- 1 teaspoon chopped rosemary
- 1/2 teaspoon honey
- 1 teaspoon lemon juice
- 1/4 teaspoon lemon zest
- 1/2 teaspoon salt (or to taste)
- 1/4 teaspoon red pepper flakes
- 1 cup Panko bread crumbs
- 3 tablespoon walnuts
- 2-3 tablespoons extra virgin oil
- 1 lb. salmon fillet, skinless

PREPARATION

1. Set the oven to 425 °F.

2. Use parchment or wax paper to line a big baking sheet.

3. Mix the mustard, rosemary, lemon zest, garlic, lemon juice, honey, red pepper flakes, and salt in a separate bowl.

4. Combine the oil, walnuts, and panko in a different small bowl.

5. Place each salmon filet on the sheet pan.

6. Season the filet with the mustard mixture.

7. Coat the panko mixture on top and press so the mixture sticks to the filet. Spray the top using cooking oil.

8. Bake the fish for between 8 and 12 minutes.

9. Serve fresh with squeezed lemon juice.

GREEK RED LENTIL SOUP

Your taste buds will be astonished (or explode) by this creamy red lentil soup served in the Greek style. Red lentils are blended with sweet carrots, garlic, and onion in a tomato-based broth. It's a perfect appetizer and works great for a mid-day snack or lunch during your diet.

Total time: 33 minutes
Per Serving: 94 calories; carbohydrates 20g; protein 7g; total fat 1.5g

INGREDIENTS

- 3 tablespoon extra virgin olive oil
- 1 large onion
- 3 garlic cloves
- 2 carrots
- 1 cup crushed tomatoes
- 2 cups red lentils
- ½ teaspoon salt (or to taste)
- 1 teaspoon rosemary
- 1 1/2 teaspoon cumin
- 3 teaspoon oregano
- 2 dry bay leaves
- 1 lemon zest
- 2 tablespoons of lemon juice
- 1/2 teaspoon of pepper flakes

PREPARATION

1. Heat about three tablespoons of extra virgin olive oil.

2. Toss in garlic, onions, and carrots. Cook for three to four minutes.

3. Add bay leaves and spices. Stir as you cook so the spices don't burn.

4. Put in the lentils, broth, and smashed tomatoes. Season using kosher salt. When the lentils are completely cooked, bring to a boil, then reduce the heat, and simmer for 15 to 20 minutes.

5. Take the soup off the heat. If you have the time, let the soup cool before blending it with an immersion blender. To achieve the desired creamy consistency, pulse a few times.

6. Toss in lemon zest, juice, and fresh parsley.

7. After transferring the soup to serving bowls, top with some extra virgin olive oil.

EGGPLANT AND CHICKPEAS

All the nutrition you need can be found in this simple yet flavorful vegan eggplant meal with chickpeas and tomatoes. You'll love the Greek flavors because they're enhanced by a small amount of extra virgin olive oil and a blend of warm spices like oregano, paprika, and cinnamon.

Total time: 60 minutes
Per serving: 144 calories; carbohydrates 26g; protein 5g; total fat 5g

INGREDIENTS

- 1.5 lbs. eggplant
- 1/2 teaspoon salt (or to taste)
- 1/2 teaspoon black pepper
- 1 medium onion
- 1 green bell pepper
- 1 medium-sized carrot
- 6 cloves of garlic, minced
- 1-1 ½ teaspoon sweet paprika
- 1 teaspoon organic ground coriander
- 3/4 teaspoon ground cinnamon
- 400g can of chickpeas (save the water)
- 400g can of chopped tomatoes

PREPARATION

1. Heat the oven to 400°F.

2. Salt the eggplant cubes and place them in a colander over a big bowl or your sink. To let the bitterness of the eggplant "sweat out," leave it alone for about 20 minutes. Towel dry after rinsing with water.

3. Heat 1/4 cup of extra virgin olive oil in a big braising pan until it's hot.

4. Add chopped carrots, pepper, and onion.

5. Toss in the garlic, bay leaf, spices, and a pinch of salt after cooking for two to three minutes while stirring often.

6. Cook for an additional minute until the spices give off an aromatic smell.

7. Add the tomato, chickpeas, and saved liquid from the chickpeas at this point.

8. Bring to a boil for ten minutes. Keep on stirring to avoid the mixture from burning at the bottom.

9. Remove from the stovetop. Cover the pan and transfer to the oven.

10. Cook for 45 minutes until the eggplant is tender.

11. Serve fresh.

SMOKED MOZZARELLA WITH ZUCCHINI LASAGNA ROLLS

In this nutritious variation on lasagna rolls, zucchini strips are used instead of lasagna noodles to create a family-friendly meal packed with vegetables. Kids will love helping with this recipe; let them get their hands dirty when rolling the cheesy zucchini ribbons. Enjoy a delicious and nutritious meal packed into strips.

Total time: 60 minutes
Per serving: 315 calories; carbohydrates 16.8g; protein 22.2g; total fat 18.6g

INGREDIENTS

- 2 large zucchinis
- 2 tablespoons extra virgin olive oil
- 1/2 teaspoon ground pepper
- 1/4 teaspoon salt
- 1 garlic clove
- 1 handful of frozen spinach
- 3/4 cup low-sodium marinara sauce
- 8 tablespoons of mozzarella cheese, shredded ad smoked
- 1 egg
- 3 tablespoons of parmesan cheese
- 1 1/3 cups part-skim ricotta
- 2 tablespoons fresh basil

PREPARATION

1. Preheat the oven to 425°F.

2. Use cooking spray to coat two rimmed baking sheets.

3. Slice the zucchini lengthwise, making a total of 1/8-inch thick 24 strips.

4. In a big bowl, combine the oil, 1/4 teaspoon of pepper, and 1/8 teaspoon of salt. Place the zucchini on the prepared pans in a single layer.

5. Bake the zucchini for 10 minutes.

6. In the meantime, mix one tablespoon of parmesan and two tablespoons of mozzarella in a small bowl.

7. In a medium bowl, combine the leftover mozzarella, parmesan, pepper, and salt with the egg, ricotta, spinach, and garlic.

8. In an 8-inch square baking dish, spread 1/4 cup marinara.

9. Place one tablespoon of the ricotta mixture at the bottom of a zucchini strip and roll it up. Put it seam-side down in the baking dish. Repeat with the rest of the filling and zucchini. You can use the saved cheese mixture to top the rolls.

10. Bake the zucchini rolls for 20 minutes or until they're bubbling and have a light golden top.

11. Sprinkle with basil just before serving.

BUCKWHEAT SALAD

The Mediterranean-inspired buckwheat salad is easy and simple to prepare. It's healthy, gluten-free, vegetarian, and packed with the superfood buckwheat. This is the perfect salad to prepare for lunches throughout the week or serve as a filling light dinner.

Total time: 30 minutes
Per serving: 205 calories; carbohydrates 5g; protein 3g; total fat 20g

INGREDIENTS

- 3/4 cup uncooked buckwheat
- 3/4 cups of water
- 1 1/2 cups grape tomatoes
- 1 1/2 cups sliced cucumbers
- 1/2 cup red onion
- 1/2 cup cubed feta cheese
- 2-3 tablespoons chopped fresh parsley
- 3 tablespoon extra virgin olive oil,
- 1/2 lemon juice
- 1/4 teaspoon of black pepper
- ¼ teaspoon salt (or to taste)

PREPARATION

1. Place the rinsed buckwheat in a saucepan. Add water and a bit of salt and bring to a boil. Reduce the heat to low, cover the pot, and cook for 15 to 20 minutes. Let it get firm for about five minutes, and fluff it using a fork.

2. Rinse the buckwheat if the water hasn't been absorbed. Place aside and let it fully cool.

3. Add the onion, cucumbers, tomatoes, feta cheese, parsley, extra virgin olive oil, lemon juice, black pepper, and salt.

4. Toss to blend.

5. Serve fresh.

TUNA SALAD

Compared to traditional tuna salad, this inventive recipe uses no mayo. It's packed with crunchy vegetables, fresh herbs, and a zesty Dijon dressing made with extra virgin olive oil and lime juice.

Total time: 10 minutes
Per Serving: 194 calories; carbohydrates 6g; protein 28g; total fat 10g

INGREDIENTS

For Mustard Dressing:

- 2 1/2 teaspoon Dijon mustard
- 1 lemon zest
- 1 1/2 lemon juice
- 1/3 cup extra virgin olive oil
- 1/2 teaspoon sumac
- ¼ teaspoon kosher salt and black pepper (or to taste)
- 1/2 teaspoon crushed red pepper flakes

For Tuna Salad:

- 3 cans of tuna
- 2 1/2 celery stalks
- 1/2 cucumber

- 4-5 radishes, stems removed
- 1/2 cup pitted Kalamata olives
- 3 green onions
- 1/2 medium red onion
- 1 bunch parsley
- 10-15 fresh mint leaves

PREPARATION

1. In small steel or ceramic bowl, combine the Dijon mustard, lime juice, and zest to make the zesty mustard vinaigrette. When thoroughly mixed, add the olive oil, sumac, salt, pepper, and crushed red pepper flakes. Put aside.

2. Mix the tuna with chopped veggies, Kalamata olives, fresh parsley, and mint leaves in a large salad bowl. Stir gently.

3. Drizzle the dressing over the tuna salad. Blend to ensure the tuna salad is coated evenly with the dressing.

4. Chill for 30 minutes before serving.

MEDITERRANEAN-STYLE SALMON BURGERS

These juicy salmon burgers are to-die-for. If you've been hunting for a salmon burger, try our recipe and make a delicious Mediterranean-style salmon burger. You get a flavorful and juiciest salmon patty with just a few simple steps.

Total time: 20 minutes
Per Serving: 137 calories; carbohydrates 4.2g; protein 1g; total fat 13.9g

INGREDIENTS

- 1 1/2 lbs. skinless salmon fillet, cut into chunks
- 2 teaspoon Dijon mustard
- 2-3 tablespoons minced green onions
- 1 cup chopped fresh parsley
- 1 teaspoon ground coriander
- 1 teaspoon ground sumac
- 1/2 teaspoon sweet paprika
- 1/2 teaspoon black pepper
- 1/4 teaspoon salt (or to taste)
- 1/3 cup Italian breadcrumbs
- 1/4 cup extra virgin olive oil
- 1 tablespoon lemon juice

- 4 burger buns
- 1 red onion
- Your favorite sauces

PREPARATION

1. Put half the salmon in the food processor and process until it becomes pasty and put aside in a bowl.

2. Toss the rest of the salmon into the food processor and pulse briefly until roughly cut into small bits. Put in the bowl with pasty salmon.

3. Add the spices, parsley, minced green onions, and salt into the bowl. Combine until everything is fully incorporated. Refrigerate for about a half-hour to allow the mixture to set.

4. Take the salmon-herb mixture out of the fridge, separate it into four equal pieces, and turn them into 10-inch-thick patties.

5. Spread the bread crumbs on a flat dish. Cover each patty with breadcrumbs, and put the breaded salmon patties on a parchment-lined sheet pan.

6. Over medium-high heat, warm three tablespoons of extra virgin olive oil. Carefully place each salmon patty into the pan and cook for two to four minutes, until lightly browned on both sides.

7. Lightly sprinkle with salt as you place the cooked salmon patties onto paper towels to absorb any excess oil.

8. Put together in buns using your favorite sauces and enjoy.

ITALIAN BAKED CHICKEN

This juicy Italian baked chicken will win you over. The recipe uses chicken breast, an excellent lean protein source. A simple blend of different staple ingredients like garlic and olive oil is used for cooking this skinless chicken breast recipe. Serve this juicy, flavorful recipe with fresh parsley an basil.

Total time: 30 minutes
Per serving: 191.8 calories; carbohydrates 3.4g; protein 32.6g; total fat 5.6g

INGREDIENTS

- 2 lbs. of boneless, skinless chicken breast
- ¼ teaspoon salt and pepper (or to taste)
- 2 teaspoons of dried oregano
- 1 teaspoon of fresh thyme
- 1 teaspoon of sweet paprika
- 4 minced garlic cloves
- 3 tablespoons of extra virgin olive oil
- 1/4 lemon juice
- 1 medium red onion, thinly sliced.

- 5-6 halved tomatoes
- 3 tablespoon fresh parsley

PREPARATION

1. Preheat the oven to 425 °F.

2. Dry the chicken using a paper towel, put it into a large Ziploc bag, and hammer it using a meat mallet until the breast piece flattens. Repeat the procedure with the remaining chicken breast pieces.

3. Place the chicken in a big mixing basin or dish after seasoning it with kosher salt and pepper on both sides. Add the lemon juice, extra virgin olive oil, minced garlic, and spices. Toss in the tomatoes.

4. Place the chopped onion slices on the bottom of a large baking dish or pan that has been lightly greased. Place the seasoned chicken on top.

5. Cover the dish and bake it for 10 minutes, then uncover it and continue baking for another eight to ten minutes. Use a quick digital cooking thermometer to check that the chicken is fully done. It must measure 165 °F.

6. Take the chicken breasts out of the oven and allow them to rest for five to ten minutes before serving.

7. Sprinkle with fresh basil and parsley before serving.

BREAKFAST EGG MUFFINS

Breakfast egg muffins are the ideal breakfast to take with you because you can prepare them ahead of time and store each one separately for usage during the week. These portable muffins are rich in protein, gluten-free, and packed with delicious vegetables.

Total time: 30 minutes
Per serving: 191.8 calories; carbohydrates 1.5g; protein 10.8g; total fat 9.8g

INGREDIENTS

- 3 tablespoon extra virgin olive oil for brushing
- 1 small red bell pepper, chopped (about ¾ cup)
- 12 cherry tomatoes, halved
- 1 shallot, finely chopped
- 6-10 pitted Kalamata olives
- 4 ounces of cooked chicken or turkey
- 1/2 cup fresh parsley leaves
- ¼ cup of crumbled feta cheese
- 8 large eggs
- ¼ teaspoon salt and pepper
- 1/2 teaspoon paprika
- 1/4 teaspoon ground turmeric
- Fresh oregano or basil for garnishing

PREPARATION

1. Place the rack in the middle of the oven and heat it to 350°F.

2. Grease a 12-cup muffin pan with oil.

3. Add peppers, olives, tomatoes, shallots, chicken, parsley, and crumbled feta to a big bowl. Combine all the ingredients.

4. Crack all the eggs into a bowl and add salt, pepper, and spices. Whisk thoroughly.

5. Carefully pour the egg mixture into the muffing pan.

6. Put a sheet pan on top of a muffin pan and bake for 25 minutes.

7. Once the top is golden, remove the pan from the oven and let it cool.

8. Loosen each muffin's edges using a small butter knife.

9. Serve with fresh oregano or basil.

CHARRED SHRIMP, PESTO, AND QUINOA BOWLS

It takes barely twenty minutes to half an hour to prepare these shrimp, pesto, and quinoa bowls. The recipes are delicious and packed with nutrition. You're welcome to add more vegetables and substitute chicken, beef, tofu, or edamame for the shrimp.

Total time: 30 minutes
Per serving: 429 calories; carbohydrates 29.3 g; protein 30.9g; total fat 23.9 g

INGREDIENTS

- 1 lb. shrimp
- 4 cups arugula
- 2 cups prepared quinoa
- 1 cup cherry tomatoes, halved
- 1 diced avocado
- 1/3 cup of pesto
- 2 tablespoon balsamic vinegar
- 1 tablespoon extra-
  virgin olive oil,
- 1/4 teaspoon ground pepper
- 1/4 teaspoon salt

PREPARATION

1. Combine pesto, vinegar, oil, salt, and pepper in a big bowl. Take four tablespoons of the mixture from the bowl and put it aside.

2. Heat a big cast-iron skillet. Add the shrimp and stir-fry for four to five minutes until just cooked with a little char. Take it out onto a platter.

3. Toss the quinoa and arugula with the vinaigrette in a sizable bowl. Divide it among four plates. Add tomatoes, avocado, and shrimp on top.

4. Drizzle each bowl with one tablespoon of the pesto mixture.

5. Serve fresh.

BREAD CHIA PUDDING

Chia seeds contain fiber, iron, and calcium and are a good source of beneficial omega-3 fatty acids that help lower your blood pressure. They also contain quercetin, which is an antioxidant known for reducing the risk of developing different heart conditions. This recipe combines chia seeds with a fruity base. The dish then sits in the refrigerator for a couple of hours to form a thick and creamy consistency.

Total time: 5 minutes
Refrigerating time: 8 hours
Per serving: 343 calories; carbohydrates 33.4g; protein 7.3g; total fat 18.1g

INGREDIENTS

- 1 3/4 cups blackberries, raspberries, and diced mango (fresh or frozen), divided

- 1 cup of milk of choice

- 1/4 cup chia seeds

- 1 tablespoon pure maple syrup

- 3/4 teaspoon vanilla extract

- 1/2 cup whole-milk plain Greek yogurt

- 1/4 cup granola

PREPARATION

1. Blend the milk and 1 1/4 cups of fruit until completely smooth.

2. Mix chia, syrup, and vanilla into the milk and fruit mixture after scraping it into a medium bowl.

3. Layer each serving of pudding with 1/4 cup of the remaining fruit, 1/4 cup yogurt, and two tablespoons of granola. Divide the pudding into two dishes.

4. Chill for eight hours.

MEDITERRANEAN STRATA

This flexible and simple Mediterranean breakfast stratum has sun-dried tomatoes, kalamata olives, mozzarella, artichoke hearts, and parmesan, making it a versatile dish with no boundaries. The recipe can also be used for dinner and is very easy to make.

Total time: 75 minutes
Per serving: 180 calories; carbohydrates 12.5g; protein 7g; total fat 9.5g

INGREDIENTS

- 3 tablespoons of butter
- 2 cloves of garlic
- 2 shallots
- 1 cup button mushrooms
- 1 teaspoon dried marjoram leaves
- 6 cups of white bread
- 1/4 cup shredded parmesan cheese
- 1 cup fresh mozzarella cheese balls
- 1/2 cup artichoke hearts
- 1/4 cup kalamata olives
- 1/4 cup tomatoes
- ¼ teaspoon salt
- 6 eggs
- 1/4 cup basil leaves

PREPARATION

1. Melt one tablespoon of butter to brush four one-cup baking plates. You can brush the inside of a two-quart baking dish if you're serving it to the family.

2. Preheat the oven to 325°F.

3. Melt two tablespoons of remaining butter in a large skillet over medium heat. Add garlic and shallot and sauté for two minutes.

4. Stir in the marjoram and mushrooms—Cook for four minutes.

5. Take the pan off the stove or heat and whisk in the bread cubes, artichoke hearts, sun-dried tomatoes, kalamata olives, parmesan, salt, and fresh mozzarella. Toss the mixture in a bowl.

6. Distribute the ingredients between four pans.

7. Whisk the eggs and equally pour one cup of the egg mixture over the bread in each serving dish.

8. Bake for almost 50 minutes or until the eggs are set.

9. Remove the strata from the oven and allow it to rest for five minutes before serving.

TAHINI DATE BANANA SHAKE

This shake recipe is perfect for an afternoon treat; you can make it in less than 5 minutes. It includes unsweetened almond milk with hints of cinnamon that combine to taste like a dreamy dessert while on a diet.

Total time: 5 minutes
Per serving: 299 calories; carbohydrates 47.7g; protein 5.7g; total fat 12.4g

INGREDIENTS

- 2 frozen sliced bananas

- 4 pitted Medjool dates

- 1 pinch of ground cinnamon

- 1/4 cup tahini

- 1/4 cup crushed ice

- 1 1/2 cups unsweetened almond milk

PREPARATION

1. Toss all the ingredients and the frozen banana slices in a blender and run it on high speed.

2. Run the blender until you the texture of the shake turns creamy.

3. Pour the banana-date shakes into serving cups and add some extra ground cinnamon.

4. Serve fresh and enjoy.

SHAKSHUKA

Shakshuka is a straightforward dish made from gently poached eggs in a tasty chunky tomato and bell pepper sauce. It's packed with nutrition and has several antioxidants, vitamins, and minerals. Once you taste this dish, you'll never go back to traditional egg breakfast again.

Total time: 30 minutes
Per serving: 111 calories; carbohydrates 9g; protein 6g; total fat 8g

INGREDIENTS

- 1/2 teaspoon ground cumin
- 1 pinch of red pepper flakes, optional
- ¼ teaspoon salt and pepper
- 6 medium tomatoes
- 1/2 cup tomato sauce
- 6 large eggs
- 2 tablespoons of olive oil
- 1 large yellow onion chopped
- 2 green chopped peppers
- 2 cloves of chopped garlic
- 1 teaspoon ground coriander
- 1 teaspoon sweet paprika
- 1/4 cup chopped fresh parsley leaves
- 1/4 cup chopped fresh mint leaves

PREPARATION

1. In a big cast iron skillet, heat three tablespoons of olive oil. Add the green peppers, onions, garlic, spices, salt, and pepper. Cook for about five minutes, stirring periodically, or until the vegetables are tender.

2. Add the chopped tomatoes and tomato sauce. Simmer for around 15 minutes on medium heat.

3. Remove the lid and cook the mixture a little longer until it thickens.

4. Use a wooden spoon to make six wells in the tomato mixture. Crack an egg into each well.

5. Cook the eggs on low heat with the lid on until they're set.

6. Remove the lid and stir in the mint and parsley. If you'd like, increase the amount of black or red pepper flakes.

7. Serve with your preferred bread, challah, or warm pita.

BABA GANOUSH

This is the best baba ganoush you'll ever try. It's an extraordinary creamy, rich, smokey eggplant dip flavored with tahini, garlic, and lemon juice.

Total time: 35 minutes
Per serving: 86.6 calories; carbohydrates 8.6g; protein 3g; total fat 8.4g

INGREDIENTS

- 2 Italian eggplants or small globe eggplants
- 1 tablespoon lemon juice
- 1 garlic clove, minced
- 1 tablespoon plain Greek yogurt (optional)
- ¼ teaspoon kosher salt and black pepper
- 1/4 cup tahini paste
- 1 teaspoon sumac
- 3/4 teaspoon Aleppo pepper or red pepper flakes
- 3 tablespoons of olive oil
- Toasted pine nuts for garnishing

PREPARATION

1. Turn your gas burner to medium-high and put the eggplant over it.

2. Turn the eggplant using a pair of tongs approximately every five minutes until it's soft and the skin is crispy and blackened on all sides.

3. After taking the eggplant off the heat, place it in a colander over a basin. Give it time to set and drain completely.

4. Place the cooked, completely drained, and bowl-ready eggplant. Use a fork to tear it into smaller pieces.

5. Add the Greek yogurt (if using), tahini paste, garlic, lemon juice, sumac, Aleppo pepper, or crushed red pepper flakes into the eggplant. Gently mix ingredients with a fork or a wooden spoon.

6. Serve fresh with toasted pine nuts.

FISH STICKS

Simple handmade fish sticks that are crisp on the outside and deliciously soft on the inside. This recipe uses Salmon to give more nutrition, but you can use any type of fish you like. The crust is a delish parmesan coating with hints of lemon zest, giving it the perfect sweet and savory balance.

Total time: 25 minutes
Per serving: 119 calories; carbohydrates 8g; protein 13.6g; total fat 3.8g

INGREDIENTS

- 1 1/2 lbs. salmon skin removed fish fillet(or any other fish)
- 1 teaspoon ground black pepper
- 1 teaspoon sweet paprika
- 1 teaspoon dried oregano
- 1/2 cup flour
- 1 beaten egg
- 1/2 bread crumbs
- 1/2 cup parmesan
- 1 lemon zest
- ½ tablespoon of lemon juice
- Parsley for garnishing

PREPARATION

1. Heat the oven to 450°F.

2. Dry the fish fillet using paper towels before seasoning both sides with salt. Slice the fish fillet to make fish sticks.

3. Combine paprika, dried oregano, and black pepper in a small bowl. Apply the spice mixture to season both sides of the fish sticks.

4. Prepare a dredging facility by putting flour in a small bowl. Next to the flour dish, crack the egg wash in a larger bowl or dish.

5. Combine the bread crumbs, parmesan cheese, and lemon zest on a separate plate. Place next to the egg wash-coated dish.

6. Take a fish stick, cover it on both sides with flour, and brush off the extra.

7. Next, coat the fish stick with egg wash before dipping it in the bread crumb-parmesan mixture. Repeat this step until all the fish sticks are breaded.

8. On an oiled baking sheet, arrange the coated fish sticks. Apply extra virgin olive oil to the fish sticks' tops.

9. Set the baking sheet on the center rack of the preheated oven.

10. Bake for 12 to 15 minutes. If the fish sticks still need to be colored, briefly broil them until they turn a lovely golden-brown color.

11. Remove the baking dish from the oven.

12. Drizzle the fish sticks with lemon juice and zest. Sprinkle with parsley and serve with your favorite dipping sauce.

MEDITERRANEAN QUINOA SALAD

This nutritious Mediterranean quinoa salad with feta makes for an easy lunch or dinner thanks to staple ingredients found in your kitchen, like chickpeas, roasted red bell peppers, and Kalamata olives. It is a light yet satisfying vegetarian meal with much nutrition and flavor.

Total time: 40 minutes
Per serving: 310 calories; carbohydrates 45g; protein 10g; total fat 12g

INGREDIENTS

- 1 1/2 cups dry quinoa
- 1/2 teaspoon salt
- ¼ teaspoon black pepper
- 1/2 cup extra virgin olive oil
- 1 tablespoon balsamic vinegar
- 2 garlic cloves, minced
- 1/2 teaspoon dried basil
- 1/2 teaspoon dried thyme
- 3 cups arugula
- 1 can of garbanzo beans
- 1 small jar of roasted red bell peppers
- 1/4 cup Kalamata olives

- 1/4 cup crumbled feta cheese

PREPARATION

1. Prepare the quinoa as listed on the package. Add half a teaspoon of salt. Remove from the stove and let it cool.

2. Combine the basil, thyme, squeezed garlic, balsamic vinegar, and olive oil in a bowl. Mix thoroughly by whisking. Add freshly ground black pepper and salt to the herbs and spice mixture. Set aside.

3. Combine the quinoa, garbanzo beans, arugula, roasted red peppers, Kalamata olives, and feta cheese in a large bowl.

4. Take the spice mixture and combine it with the quinoa in a large bowl.

5. Add basil for garnishing and serve at room temperature.

CHICKEN WRAP

This delicious, quick Mediterranean chicken wrap is packed with the tastiest ingredients. It offers so much diversity in terms of flavor, filled with spicy chicken and a delicious yogurt sauce with hints of garlic. The vegetables add a fresh flavor that combines with the hummus to give an epic and tasty meal.

Total time: 30 minutes
Per serving: 488 calories; carbohydrates 35g; protein 58g; total fat 11g

INGREDIENTS

- 1 ½ lbs. chicken breast, skinned and boneless

- 1 tablespoon olive oil

- 1 teaspoon chili flakes

- 1 teaspoon ground black pepper

- 3 cloves of minced garlic

- ½ cup yogurt

- Salt to taste

- Hummus

- 1 cup of chopped cabbage

- Salad

- 3-4 tortillas

PREPARATION

1. Prepare a salad from the vegetables of your choice.

2. Prepare the yogurt sauce by mixing the 1 clove of minced garlic, yogurt, and a pinch of salt. The mixture should be well-combined.

3. Chop the chicken breast into small cubes and set aside.

4. Take a pan and heat the olive oil. Add in the chicken cubes and cook on medium-high heat.

5. Add the remaining two cloves of garlic, pepper, and chili flakes, and stir until the chicken turns tender. It would take about 8 to 10 minutes for the chicken to turn golden.

6. Heat the tortillas during this time.

7. Assemble your wrap by placing the chicken, some hummus, salad, yogurt paste, and any other dressing you like. Wrap the tortilla with the filling inside and enjoy.

EGG CAPRESE BREAKFAST CUPS

Eggs for breakfast never get old. This recipe only takes two minutes in the oven and is perfect for busy mornings when you need a nutritional breakfast to start your day. The cheese topping and tomatoes add a lot of flavors, making it an incredibly tasty breakfast.

Total time: 7 minutes
Per serving: 262 calories; carbohydrates 1g; protein 23g; total fat 18g

INGREDIENTS

- 1/3 cup shredded mozzarella
- 2 eggs
- 2 pieces of thinly cut ham
- 1 teaspoon pesto
- 3 cherry tomatoes, sliced in half
- ¼ teaspoon black pepper
- ¼ teaspoon salt (or to taste)
- 2 basil leaves (optional)

PREPARATION

1. Brush a ramekin with olive oil and layer it with ham slices and cheese.

2. Crack the eggs into the ramekins, top with a dollop of pesto and a few cherry tomatoes, and season with black pepper and kosher salt.

3. Cook on high for 90 seconds or until the whites are set.

4. Garnish with additional black pepper, salt, and basil leaves if preferred.

5. Serve fresh.

MEDITERRANEAN EGG CASSEROLE

This egg casserole dish is perfect for a healthy breakfast for the whole family. It's packed with fresh herbs, ricotta cheese, and broccoli to deliver a flavorful and nutritional meal. You can make your own version of this casserole by substituting the ingredients.

Total Time: 1 hour 10 minutes
Per Serving: 188 calories; carbohydrates 13g; protein 11g; total fat 11g

INGREDIENTS

- 8 ounces whole mushrooms, sliced
- 2 medium diced sweet potatoes
- 1 diced red bell pepper
- 1 small head of broccoli, only florets
- 1 diced red onion
- Salt and pepper to taste
- 3 tablespoons olive oil
- ½ cup milk
- 12 large eggs
- 1 clove of minced garlic
- 1 ½ teaspoon mixed herbs
- 4 ounces ricotta cheese
- Fresh basil and thyme for garnishing

PREPARATION

1. Preheat the oven to 400 F and place the racks in the upper and lower thirds of your oven.

2. Lightly grease a 9 x 13-inch casserole dish and keep aside.

3. Prepare two large baking sheets and lightly grease them too.

4. Place all the vegetables in a large bowl and season with salt, pepper, and olive oil. Toss the bowl to coat completely.

5. Divide the vegetables into two equal portions and spread them on the baking sheets in a single layer—cake for 20 minutes at the same temperature.

6. Keep on tossing the vegetables to cook them thoroughly.

7. Layer half of the vegetables in the casserole dish and reduce the temperature to 350 F.

8. Take a large bowl and beat the milk, eggs, and garlic. Pour the egg mixture into the casserole dish.

9. Spread the remaining vegetables on the top. Spread the ricotta cheese on top.

10. Place the dish in the oven and bake for 35 to 40 minutes or until the top turns golden.

11. Serve warm with fresh basil and thyme.

SHRIMP SCAMPI PASTA WITH ZUCCHINI NOODLES

The perfect midweek dinner comprises healthy spiralized zucchini combined with a shrimp scampi with hints of garlic and whole wheat linguine pasta. Enjoy all the flavors in every bite that offers nutrition and taste at the same time.

Total time: 40 minutes
Per serving: 521 calories; carbohydrates 52g; protein 28g; total fat 22g

INGREDIENTS

- 1 lb. large shrimp
- 1 12-ounce package of organic wheat linguine
- 4 large cloves of minced garlic
- 1/3 cup + 2 tablespoon olive oil
- ¼ teaspoon salt
- ¼ teaspoon black pepper
- 3 zucchinis, medium-sized
- 3 tablespoons of butter
- 1 teaspoon red chili flakes
- 3 tablespoons of lemon juice
- 1/2 cup parmesan cheese, grated

PREPARATION

1. After completely cleaning the shrimp and devein them, put them aside in a medium bowl.

2. Season the shrimp with minced garlic, salt, and pepper.

3. Cut the end of the zucchinis and make noodles using a spiralizer. Using a knife, you can also use a vegetable peeler to make long ribbons or simply slice them into long ribbons.

4. Boil water in a large pot and add salt to taste. To ensure the linguine fully cooks, follow the instructions on the package, and take them off 2 minutes before the cooking time prescribed on the package.

5. Transfer the cooked linguine to a colander and save the pasta water.

6. Add a tablespoon of olive oil to a skillet and heat.

7. Place the shrimp in the skillet, and cook for two minutes. Flip the shrimp over, and cook for an additional two minutes or till the outside of the shrimp turns opaque.

8. Put the shrimp on a platter.

9. Heat the remaining 1/3 cup of olive oil and the butter in the same pan over medium to high heat.

10. Remove the chunks of garlic and add the remaining two minced cloves, red chili (flakes), lemon juice, lemon zest, and 1/2 cup of the pasta water set aside.

11. Add the zucchini noodles to the pasta water in the pan and heat for one minute while stirring to cook the rawness.

12. Strain out the noodles and add them to the olive oil mixture. Toss to combine with the linguine noodles and 1/4 cup of the Parmesan cheese.

13. Season the pasta, zucchini, and shrimp to taste with additional salt and black pepper. Add the last 1/4 cup of parmesan cheese on top.

14. Serve warm.

VEGAN STUFFED BELL PEPPERS

These bell peppers are delicious and healthy because they are filled with rice and vegetables. This dish might be ideal if you seek a reliable, simple, and delicious weeknight supper option.

Total time: 50 minutes
Per serving: 155 calories; carbohydrates 15.2g; protein 6.6g; total fat 8.2g

INGREDIENTS

- 3/4 cup whole grain uncooked brown rice
- 6 medium bell peppers
- 2-3 tablespoons of olive oil
- 3/4 cup of chopped fresh parsley
- 3/4 cup tomato puree
- 2 small diced onions
- 1 cup of sliced cremini mushrooms
- 2 small sliced carrots
- 1 small zucchini cut into cubes
- 1 pinch of chili powder
- Salt and pepper to taste

PREPARATION

1. Preheat the oven to 425°F.

2. Cook the brown rice as stated on the package in a small pan over medium heat. Drain and set aside.

3. Remove the tops of the bell peppers and scoop out the seeds. Carefully wash the peppers and set them aside.

4. Heat olive oil in a large pan. Add in the onion and sauté it for two to three minutes or until tender.

5. Add the mushrooms and fry them for five to eight minutes.

6. Once the mushrooms are half-cooked, add the zucchini and carrots. Cook for another five minutes, stirring occasionally.

7. Remove the pan from heat.

8. Mix the cooked rice, tomato purée, and 1/3 cup parsley.

9. Add salt, pepper, and a dash of red chili powder to season.

10. After dividing the mixture, put the "lids" on the peppers.

11. Place the filled peppers in a greased baking dish.

12. Bake for around 20 to 25 minutes or until the edges start to turn golden-brown.

13. Garnish with parsley and serve warm.

MEDITERRANEAN TURKEY BURGERS

Tender, juicy, and delicious turkey burgers from the Mediterranean region. They are bursting with traditional Mediterranean flavors like fresh dill, garlic, and lemon juice that will have everyone asking for more.

Total time: 50 minutes
Per serving: 516 calories; carbohydrates 42.9g; protein 28.6g; total fat 23.9g

INGREDIENTS

For Burger Patties:

- 3 tablespoon olive oil, divided
- 2 tablespoons fresh dill, finely chopped
- 1 teaspoon freshly squeezed lemon juice (from half a lemon)
- 1/2 teaspoon ground cumin
- 1/2 teaspoon salt
- 1/4 teaspoon black pepper
- 1 medium onion, diced
- 1 tablespoon garlic, minced
- 1 lb. ground turkey
- 1/2 cup breadcrumbs

For Burger Toppings:

- 4 hamburger buns
- 4 slices of tomato
- 4 pieces of lettuce
- Sauces of choice

PREPARATION

1. Heat two tablespoons of olive oil in a large skillet for two minutes over medium-high heat.

2. Add the onions and garlic. Sauté until they are soft and well browned. Remove from the pan.

3. Put the breadcrumbs, dill, lemon juice, cumin, salt, and pepper in a large mixing bowl along with the ground turkey, sautéed onion, and garlic. Mix using a spatula.

4. Refrigerate the turkey mixture for 30 minutes or overnight to help it retain its shape.

5. Use your hands to form four equal portions of the turkey mixture into balls. Pat the balls into patties by pressing them flat between your palms.

6. Heat the leftover tablespoon of olive oil in a cast-iron skillet over medium-high heat.

7. Place the patties on the skillet and cook for three to five minutes until nicely seared and brown on the sides.

8. Flip the patties over and cook on low heat for another three to five minutes.

9. Slice the buns, place a turkey patty on each, and add lettuce.

10. Top the patty with tomato.

11. Layer using your favorite sauces and serve warm

SAUCY GREEK BAKED SHRIMP

This delicious, nutritious shrimp meal with feta and tomato sauce may be prepared as a one-pot dinner or as a quick and simple appetizer that is always the first thing to go.

Total time: 35 minutes
Per serving: 280 calories; carbohydrates 12g; protein 28g; total fat 17g

INGREDIENTS

- 1 lb. large, deveined shrimp
- 1 medium onion
- 3 garlic cloves
- 1 15-ounce can of crushed tomatoes
- 1/2 teaspoon red pepper flakes
- 1/4 teaspoon salt
- 2 tablespoons chopped fresh dill
- 1/2 teaspoon ground allspice
- 1/2 teaspoon ground cinnamon
- 3 tablespoons of olive oil
- 1/2 cup crumbled feta cheese

PREPARATION

1. Preheat the oven to 375°F.

2. Place the cleaned, dried shrimp in a basin. After seasoning with kosher salt and red pepper flakes, set it aside.

3. Heat olive oil in a large, heavy skillet over medium-high heat.

4. Sauté the onion and garlic for five minutes or until tender. Add the spices and simmer for 30 seconds.

5. Add the tomatoes and cook for 20 minutes, stirring occasionally.

6. Remove from the heat, add the shrimp to the tomato sauce, and top with crumbled feta cheese.

7. Bake the shrimp for 15 to 18 minutes or until they are fully cooked.

8. Serve warm with bread.

ONE-POT LENTILS

One-pot lentils cooked in about 20 minutes are wholesome, filling, and tasty. They are quick to prepare in a few easy steps, seasoned, and cooked till tender to add flavor.

Total time: 20 minutes
Per serving: 183 calories; carbohydrates 32.1g; protein 12.1g; total fat 1.4g

INGREDIENTS

- 1 ½ cup dry brown lentils
- 1/8 cup olive oil
- 1/4 teaspoon turmeric
- 1/2 teaspoon cumin seeds
- 1/2 teaspoon Italian seasoning
- 1/2 teaspoon salt
- 1/4 teaspoon freshly ground black pepper
- 1/2 cup chopped onion
- 1 minced garlic clove

PREPARATION

1. Drain, rinse, and add the lentils to a large mixing basin. Let it sit for 10 minutes after adding hot water to the top. Set aside.

2. Heat oil over medium heat in a four-quart Dutch oven. Add turmeric, onions, and garlic.

3. Sauté for three minutes and add one cup of boiling water to the pot.

4. Drain the lentils.

5. Add the remaining boiling water, Italian seasoning, cumin, salt, lentils, and pepper to the pot. Bring to a boil.

6. Lower the heat to low-medium, cover the pot and simmer for 15 minutes.

7. Add additional salt and pepper to the pot.

8. Garnish with fresh cilantro.

9. Serve on top of white or brown rice, coconut rice, or pilaf.

AVOCADO CAPRESE WRAP

This avocado Caprese wrap is quick, easy, and healthful to make, and it is the ideal size for a celebration lunch for a large group or a quick snack for one.

Total time: 6 minutes
Per serving: 154 calories; carbohydrates 17g; protein 3g; total fat 9g

INGREDIENTS

- 2 whole wheat tortillas
- 2 tablespoon olive oil
- 1 teaspoon balsamic vinegar
- 1/4 teaspoon salt
- 1/4 teaspoon black pepper
- 1/2 cup of fresh arugula leaves
- 1 sliced avocado
- ½ cup fresh sliced mozzarella cheese
- 1 tomato
- 6 basil leaves

PREPARATION

1. Put tomato, mozzarella cheese, and avocado on the bottom third of the tortilla.

2. Sprinkle with a few torn-up basil leaves and toss some balsamic vinegar and olive oil over the top.

3. Add kosher salt and pepper to taste.

4. Serve the tortilla folded into thirds.

GRILLED TILAPIA

This grilled tilapia is delicious and simple to prepare. The level of flavor in this nutritious meal preparation will wow you.

Total time: 23 minutes
Per serving: 145 calories; carbohydrates 2g; protein 30g; total fat 3g

INGREDIENTS

- 4 4-ounce tilapia fillets
- 1 tablespoon olive oil
- 2 teaspoon smoked paprika
- 1/2 teaspoon garlic powder
- 1/2 teaspoon onion powder
- 1/8 teaspoon celery seeds
- 1 teaspoon salt
- 1/2 teaspoon freshly ground pepper

PREPARATION

1. Bring a grill to a medium-high temperature.

2. Dry the tilapia using a paper towel. Season it with olive oil, salt, and pepper.

3. Season the fish with smoked paprika, onion powder, celery seeds, and garlic powder.

4. Grill the tilapia over indirect heat until it releases from the grill grate for 3 to 4 minutes.

5. Cook for a further three to four minutes on the other side until the tilapia gives an internal temperature of 130 to 140 degrees Fahrenheit.

6. Serve warm with blistered tomatoes.

14-Day Meal Plan

Do you wish to begin eating like a Greek? Here's a 14-day meal plan to jumpstart your new diet.

Day 1

Breakfast: Muffin-Tin Quiches with Smoked Cheddar and Potato
Per Serving: 238 calories; carbohydrates 10.8g; protein 13.6g; total fat 15.3g

INGREDIENTS

- 2 tablespoons extra virgin olive oil
- 1 1/2 cups of red-skinned potatoes
- 1 cup diced red onion
- 3/4 teaspoon salt, divided
- 8 large eggs
- 1/2 cup low-fat milk
- 1/2 teaspoon ground black pepper
- 11/2 cups of fresh spinach
- 1 cup shredded smoked cheddar

PREPARATION

1. Preheat the oven to 325°F.

2. Coat a 12-cup muffin tin with oil.

3. Boil the potatoes with the onion and 1/4 teaspoon salt until they are barely tender, about five minutes.

4. Take the pan off the stove and give it five minutes to cool.

5. In a big bowl, combine eggs, cheese, milk, pepper, and the last 1/2 teaspoon of salt.

6. Add spinach and the potato mixture after mixing.

7. Distribute the quiche ingredients among the muffin tins as desired.

8. Bake for almost 25 minutes or until the mixture feels firm.

9. Remove from the heat, and let it cool for five minutes.

10. Serve right away!

Lunch : Buckwheat Salad (See page 32)

Dinner: Chicken Wrap (See page 58)

Day 2

Breakfast: Egg Caprese Breakfast Cups (See page 60)

Lunch: Vegan Stuffed Bell peppers (See page 67)

Dinner: Mediterranean Flounder
Per Serving: 282 calories; carbohydrates 8.2g; protein 24.4g; total fat 15.4g

---

INGREDIENTS

- 5 Roma tomatoes
- 2 tablespoons extra virgin olive oil
- ½ Spanish onion
- 2 cloves of garlic
- 24 Kalamata olives,
- 1/4 cup white wine
- 1 pinch of Italian seasoning
- 1/4 cup capers
- 1 lb. flounder fillets
- 1 teaspoon fresh lemon juice
- 6 leaves of fresh basil, chopped
- 3 tablespoon freshly grated parmesan cheese

- 6 fresh basil leaves

PREPARATION

1. Preheat the oven to 425°F.

2. Bring the water in a pot to a boil. Put the tomatoes in the boiling water for a few seconds, then take them out and place them in icy water. Drain the tomatoes and remove their skins. Chop the tomatoes and set them aside.

3. Heat olive oil in a skillet. Add onions, and cook for five minutes.

4. Toss in the tomatoes, garlic, and Italian seasoning and stir, cooking for five to seven minutes or until the tomatoes are soft.

5. Add the lemon juice, capers, olives, wine, and half of the basil into the tomato mixture. Cook them for around 12 to 15 minutes on low heat, stirring in the parmesan cheese along the way.

6. Put the flounder in a small baking dish and sprinkle the remaining basil leaves on top.

7. Bake the fish for about ten minutes or until tender.

8. Remove the fish from the oven, place it on a plate, and pour some tomato sauce on top.

9. Serve immediately.

Day 3

Breakfast: Caprese Avocado Toast

Per Serving: 329 calories; carbohydates 25g; protein 12 g; total fat 22g

---

INGREDIENTS

- 1 slice of whole-wheat toast

- 1-2 teaspoon flaxseed oil

- 1/2 avocado

- 1/3 cup low-fat cottage cheese

- 1 small tomato

- 6 basil leaves

- ¼ teaspoon flaked sea salt

PREPARATION

1. Toast the bread in a bread toaster.

2. Pour some flaxseed oil on the bread.

3. Place the tomato, cottage cheese, and avocado on the toast.

4. Garnish with basil leaves, sprinkle sea salt on top, and serve right away.

Lunch: Eggplant and Chickpeas (See page 28)

Dinner: Mediterranean-Style Salmon Burgers (See page 36)

Day 4

Breakfast: Breakfast Egg Muffins (See page 40)

Lunch: No-Noodle Eggplant Lasagna
Per Serving: 301 calories; carbohydrates 19.1g; protein 24.3g; total fat 13.1g

---

INGREDIENTS

- 2 large eggplants
- 1 tablespoon extra virgin olive oil
- 12 ounces lean ground beef
- 1 cup chopped onion
- 2 clove garlic
- 1/4 cup dried wine
- 3/4 teaspoon salt
- 1 egg
- 1 cup shredded mozzarella cheese
- 6 fresh basil leaves

PREPARATION

1. Set oven to 400°F.

2. Apply cooking spray to two large baking sheets.

3. Lay the eggplant slices on the prepared pans in a single layer and roast them for 20 minutes.

4. Heat oil in a big skillet.

5. Add garlic, beef, and onion. Stir for six to eight minutes, breaking up the meat with a wooden spoon until browned.

6. Toss in the tomatoes, wine, basil, oregano, salt, and pepper. Cook for 10 minutes, occasionally stirring, until thickened.

7. Add ricotta and egg to a small bowl.

8. Spread one cup of the sauce in a 9x13-inch baking dish. Arrange 1/4 of the eggplant slices over the tomato sauce, and sprinkle with roughly 1/3 cup of the ricotta mixture and 1/4 cup of mozzarella.

9. Create a new eggplant layer and add one cup of sauce, 1/3 cup of the ricotta mixture, and 1/4 cup of mozzarella on top. Repeat the process with the remaining ingredients.

10. Bake the eggplant lasagna for about 30 to 40 minutes or until the sauce is bubbling around the edges.

11. Remove the lasagna pan from the oven and let it stand for 10 to 20 minutes.

12. Garnish with fresh basil before serving.

Dinner: Walnut-Rosemary Crusted Salmon (See page 24)

Day 5

Breakfast: Tahini Date Banana Shake (See page 48)

Lunch: Tuna Salad (See page 34)

Dinner: Chicken Shawarma

Per Serving: 320 calories; carbohydrates 4.3g; protein 39.8g; total fat 15.4g

---

INGREDIENTS

For Chicken:

- 1 + 1/2 lbs. chicken thighs or breasts, skinless and boneless
- 2 tablespoon olive oil, divided
- 2 teaspoon ground cumin
- 1 teaspoon paprika
- 1 teaspoon garlic powder
- 1 teaspoon cayenne pepper
- 1 teaspoon ground coriander
- 1 teaspoon salt
- 1/2 ground black pepper

For Shawarma Wraps:

- 6 small pita bread
- 1 medium tomato
- 2 cups romaine lettuce
- 2 Persian or mini cucumbers
- 1/4 fresh parsley

PREPARATION

1. Combine all the spices, one tablespoon of oil, and chicken strips in a bag.

2. Allow the chicken to marinade for an hour or overnight in the refrigerator.

3. Set the oven to 400°F. Place the chicken in a large half-sheet baking pan lined with parchment paper.

4. Bake the chicken for 15 to 20 minutes or until crisp and well done.

5. After taking the pan out of the oven, let it cool for ten minutes.

6. Place lettuce, tomato, cucumber, and parsley on the pita bread.

7. Put the chicken on top.

8. Serve right away!

Day 6

Breakfast: Muesli with Raspberries

Per Serving: 288 calories; carbohydrates 51.8g; protein 13g; total fat 6.6g

---

INGREDIENTS

- 1 cup of raspberries
- 1/3 cup muesli
- 3/4 cup low-fat milk

PREPARATION

Add the raspberries to the muesli and serve with milk. It's that simple!

Lunch: Baba Ganoush (See page 52)

Dinner: Zucchini Lasagna Rolls
with Smoked Mozzarella (See page 30)

Day 7

Breakfast: Hummus Toast (See page 22)

Lunch: Piled-High Vegetable Pitas
Per Serving: 399 calories; carbohydrates 52.7g; protein 15.1g; total fat 14.8g

---

INGREDIENTS

- 1 tablespoon olive oil
- 1 cup canned no-salt-added chickpeas
- 1/4 teaspoon garlic powder
- 1/2 teaspoon paprika
- 1/4 teaspoon ground cumin
- 1/8 teaspoon ground pepper
- 2 cups roasted butternut squash and root vegetables
- 1 cup fresh baby spinach
- 1 1/3 cups of mixed vegetables
- 1/2 cup cherry tomatoes, halved
- 1/4 cup crumbled reduced-fat feta cheese
- 1/2 cup hummus
- 2 pieces of pita bread

PREPARATION

1. Over medium-high heat, warm up the oil in a 10-inch skillet.

2. Add the chickpeas and season with paprika, cumin, garlic powder, and pepper.

3. Cook for almost six to eight minutes or until the chickpeas are lightly browned.

4. Remove the chickpeas from the skillet.

5. Add lemon-roasted mixed vegetables, roasted butternut squash and root vegetables, spinach, tomatoes, and feta to the chickpeas. Toss to combine.

6. Serve with lemon wedges, pita, and hummus.

Dinner: Charred Shrimp, Pesto, and Quinoa Bowls (See page 42)

Day 8

Breakfast: Mediterranean Egg Casserole (See page 62)

Lunch: Greek Red Lentil Soup (See page 26)

Dinner: Vegetarian Stuffed Eggplant
Per Serving: 511 calories; carbohydrates 72g; protein 18g; total fat 20g

INGREDIENTS

- 2 large eggplants
- 2 tablespoon + 1/4 cup extra-virgin olive oil
- 1/2 teaspoon ground cumin
- ½ teaspoon ground coriander
- 1 teaspoon smoked paprika

For the Filling:

- 2 cloves of minced garlic
- ¼ cup raisins
- 1 small diced yellow onion
- 1 diced tomato
- 1 cup dry Moroccan couscous
- 1 cup water
- 1 cup canned chickpeas, drained

- ¼ cup feta cheese, crumbled
- Chopped parsley for garnishing
- Tahini sauce for serving

PREPARATION

1. Preheat the oven to 425 ° F.

2. Slice the eggplants from top to bottom. Place the flat side up and lay them on a big pan. Sprinkle salt on top of each surface and let the eggplants sit for about 20 minutes to draw out the extra moisture.

3. Combine the cumin, coriander, and paprika in a small bowl and keep aside.

4. Dry the eggplant using a paper towel and grease the top with olive oil. Rub hald of the eggplant with the spices and roast for 35 to 40 minutes at 425 ° F.

5. Make the filling on medium high flame by sautéing the garlic and onion for about two minutes. Add the water and rasising and bring to a boil.

6. Combine the couscous and cover the pan with a lid.

7. Turn the heat off and let the mixture sit for around five minutes.

8. Use another ball to mix the cooked couscous with the chickpeas, feta cheese, the remaining spice mixture, tomatoes, and parsley. Add a bit of salt and pepper.

9. Lay the roasted eggplant on a plate and make room for the filling. Stuff the center with the couscous mixture and top with parsley and feta cheese.

10. Serve fresh with Tahini sauce

Day 9

Breakfast: Sheet Pan Baked Eggs and Vegetables (See page 20)

Lunch: Quinoa Stuffed Peppers

Per Serving: 112 calories; cabohydrates 18g; protein 5g; total fat 3g

---

INGREDIENTS

- 2 bell peppers

- 1 cup organic quinoa

- 4 garlic cloves

- 3 medium shallots

- 1/4 cup parsley

- 3/4 cup chopped pistachios

- 2 tablespoons extra
  virgin olive oil

- 1/4 teaspoon red pepper flakes

- 1 teaspoon paprika

- 1 teaspoon dried oregano

- 1/2 teaspoon sea salt

- 1/4 teaspoon black pepper

- 2 tablespoon lemon juice
  + zest from ½ lemon

- 1/4 cup feta cheese

PREPARATION

1. Preheat the oven to 425°F.

2. Discard the seeds and stems from the peppers before cutting them in half lengthwise. Place the peppers on top of a parchment-lined baking pan.

3. After 15 minutes of baking with the cut side down, turn the baking sheet over, sprinkle the peppers with salt and pepper, and remove from the oven.

4. Drain and rinse the quinoa before adding two cups of water to a pot. Bring it to a boil, lower the heat to a simmer, cover the pan, and cook for almost 15 to 20 minutes, or until all the water has been absorbed. Put the lid on and turn off the heat.

5. Mince garlic, shallot, and parsley.

6. Slice the pistachios.

7. Add two tablespoons of olive oil to a big skillet. When the onion is translucent, and the garlic is aromatic, add the garlic, shallot, and red pepper flakes and sauté for one to two minutes.

8. Turn off the heat and toss the cooked quinoa, pistachios, parsley, paprika, lemon juice, oregano, zest, sea salt, and black pepper.

9. Add a few more pinches of salt.

10. Stuff the filling into the halves of the roasted peppers, and bake for 15 minutes until tender.

11. Sprinkle the bell peppers with parsley and feta cheese crumble before serving.

Dinner: Fish Sticks (See page 54)

Day 10

Breakfast: Roasted Asparagus with Poached Eggs

Per Serving: 213 calories; carbohydrates 2.3g; protein 13.4g; total fat 16.6 g

---

INGREDIENTS

- 1 bunch asparagus, ends trimmed
- 2 tablespoon olive oil
- ¼ teaspoon ground black pepper
- 4 eggs
- 2 tablespoons white vinegar
- 1 teaspoon salt
- 1 handful of fresh dill or another herb

PREPARATION

1. Set the oven to 425°F.

2. Spray a baking sheet with cooking oil.

3. Place trimmed asparagus on the baking sheet, drizzle it with olive oil, salt, and pepper, and roast it for 12 to 15 minutes or until tender.

4. Crack each egg into a tiny bowl while the asparagus is baking, taking care not to crack the yolk.

5. Boil water in a saucepan and add vinegar. Reduce the heat once the water is simmering. Slide the eggs into the water and cook until the whites are set.

6. With a slotted spoon, carefully remove the eggs from the water.

7. Sprinkle salt and pepper on the eggs and serve them with the roasted asparagus. Garnish with fresh dill or other herbs before serving.

Lunch: Tuna Salad (See page 34)

Dinner: Avocado Caprese Wrap (See page 75)

Day 11

Breakfast: Bread Chia Pudding (See page 44)

Lunch: Mediterranean Turkey Burgers (See page 69)

Dinner: Shrimp Marinara

Per Serving: 434 calories; carbohydrates 45.8; protein 30.9g; total fat 14.3g

INGREDIENTS

For Shrimp and Pasta:

- 8 ounces spaghetti noodles
- 1 lb. large shrimp, deveined
- 2 teaspoon dried basil
- 1/4 teaspoon kosher salt
- 2 tablespoon butter
- ¼ cup parmesan cheese, for garnish

For the Marinara Sauce:

- 1 28-ounce can of crushed fire-roasted tomatoes
- 2 tablespoon olive oil
- 1 tablespoon balsamic vinegar
- 2 teaspoon garlic powder
- 1 teaspoon dried oregano

- 1 teaspoon kosher salt
- 8 fresh basil leaves

PREPARATION

1. Defrost the shrimp. When it's thawed, use a clean cloth or paper towel to pat the shrimp dry.

2. Bring a large saucepan of salted water to a boil.

3. Toss in the pasta and boil it until it's al dente. Drain it.

4. Heat butter over medium-high heat in a big skillet, and add kosher salt, basil, and shrimp.

5. Turn the shrimp using tongs after one to two minutes or until almost cooked through. Remove the shrimp and place it in a bowl.

6. Add the marinara sauce ingredients to the same skillet and whisk them together while scraping any browned bits from the bottom of the pan—Cook for 15 minutes with a lid on after bringing to a simmer.

7. Remove the skillet from the heat, and add the shrimp.

8. Serve with chopped basil and optional parmesan cheese.

Day 12

Breakfast: Fruit and Yoghurt Parfait

Per serving: 359 calories; carbohydrates 60.5g; protein 13.5g; total fat 7.8g

---

INGREDIENTS

- ½ cup Greek yogurt
- ½ cups fruit
- ½ cup granola cereal
- 1/8 cup granular sucralose sweetener

PREPARATION

1. Pour 1/4 cup of yogurt into the bottom of a tall, spherical glass and whisk well with the sweetener. Over the top, spread 1/4 cup of granola cereal.

2. Place 1/4 cup of fruit over the granola.

3. Serve with some more fresh fruit.

Lunch: One-Pot Lentils (See page 73)

Dinner: Italian Baked Chicken (See page 38)

Day 13

Breakfast: Potato Omelet Recipe

Per Serving: 176.2 calories, carbohydrates 16.4g; protein 7.7g; total fat 9.1g

INGREDIENTS

- 1 tablespoon extra virgin olive oil
- 3 gold potatoes, about 12 ounces, peeled and cut into ½-inch cubes
- 2 green onions
- 1-2 garlic cloves
- 1 teaspoon coriander
- 1 teaspoon Aleppo pepper
- 1/2 teaspoon sweet paprika
- 1/4 teaspoon turmeric
- 6 large eggs
- 1/2 cup chopped fresh dill
- ¼ teaspoon kosher salt
- 1/2 cup chopped fresh parsley

PREPARATION

1. Heat the oven to 375°F.

2. Heat two tablespoons of extra virgin olive oil over medium-high heat in 10-inch cast iron or oven-safe skillet.

3. Add garlic, green onions, and potato cubes to the skillet. Toast lighting.

4. Sprinkle kosher salt, turmeric, paprika, coriander, and Aleppo pepper. Cook for approximately five to ten minutes or until the potatoes are soft.

5. Whisk the eggs and fresh herbs together in a mixing bowl. Add a generous pinch of baking powder and kosher salt.

6. Pour the egg mixture over the potatoes. Make sure the edges and bottom settle slightly.

7. Place the skillet inside the oven. Bake for eight to ten minutes or until the eggs are completely set.

8. Remove from the oven.

9. Serve right away!

Lunch: Mediterranean Quinoa Salad (See page 56)

Dinner: Grilled Tilapia (See page 77)

Day 14

Breakfast: Challah Bread Recipe

Per Serving: 124 calories; carbohydrates 22.2g; protein 3.9g; total fat 6.5g

---

INGREDIENTS

- 2 1/4 teaspoon active dry yeast

- 1 cup of warm water

- 4 cups all-purpose flour

- 7 large egg yolks

- 1/4 cup sugar

- 1 teaspoon salt

- 6 tablespoons extra virgin olive oil

- 2-3 tablespoon toasted sesame seeds

PREPARATION

1. Combine the yeast, sugar, and warm water in a small basin. Let the yeast mixture sit for 10 minutes until it's frothy.

2. Place the flour, egg yolks, salt, and oil in a sizable mixing basin. Use a wooden spoon to stir.

3. Add the yeast mixture and stir until everything comes together.

4. Knead the dough for 10 minutes on a lightly greased surface. If the dough becomes too sticky while being worked, add a bit of flour and work the dough until it is soft and elastic.

5. Place the dough in a greased mixing bowl and let it rise for 1 1/2 hours.

6. Dust your work surface with flour, punch down the dough, and toss it on the surface.

7. Divide the dough into three equal pieces, roll it into three 16–18-inch-long ropes, and braid them.

8. Put the braided loaf on a baking sheet lined with parchment paper. Allow it to rise once more for another 30 to 45 minutes. Set the oven to 350°F in the meantime.

9. Generously brush the bread with egg white and sprinkle with sesame seeds.

10. Bake for almost 20 to 25 minutes or until golden brown.

11. Let the bread cool down before cutting yourself a slice.

Lunch: Shrimp Scampi Pasta with Zucchini Noodles (See page 64)

Dinner: Saucy Greek Baked Shrimp (See page 71)

EXCLUSIVE BONUS

40 Weight Loss Recipes

&

14 Days Meal Plan

Scan the QR-Code and receive
the FREE download:

Disclaimer

This book contains opinions and ideas of the author and is meant to teach the reader informative and helpful knowledge while due care should be taken by the user in the application of the information provided. The instructions and strategies are possibly not right for every reader and there is no guarantee that they work for everyone. Using this book and implementing the information/recipes therein contained is explicitly your own responsibility and risk. This work with all its contents, does not guarantee correctness, completion, quality or correctness of the provided information. Misinformation or misprints cannot be completely eliminated.